EVOLVE

WORKBOOK

Octavio Ramírez Espinosa

2A

CAMBRIDGE
UNIVERSITY PRESS

CAMBRIDGE
UNIVERSITY PRESS

University Printing House, Cambridge CB2 8BS, United Kingdom

One Liberty Plaza, 20th Floor, New York, NY 10006, USA

477 Williamstown Road, Port Melbourne, VIC 3207, Australia

314–321, 3rd Floor, Plot 3, Splendor Forum, Jasola District Centre, New Delhi – 110025, India

79 Anson Road, #06–04/06, Singapore 079906

Cambridge University Press is part of the University of Cambridge.

It furthers the University's mission by disseminating knowledge in the pursuit of education, learning and research at the highest international levels of excellence.

www.cambridge.org
Information on this title: www.cambridge.org/9781108408639

© Cambridge University Press 2019

First published 2019

20 19 18 17 16 15 14 13 12 11 10 9 8 7 6 5 4 3 2 1

Printed in Dubai by Oriental Press

A catalogue record for this publication is available from the British Library

ISBN 978-1-108-40524-9 Student's Book
ISBN 978-1-108-40505-8 Student's Book A
ISBN 978-1-108-40917-9 Student's Book B
ISBN 978-1-108-40526-3 Student's Book with Practice Extra
ISBN 978-1-108-40506-5 Student's Book with Practice Extra A
ISBN 978-1-108-40919-3 Student's Book with Practice Extra B
ISBN 978-1-108-40898-1 Workbook with Audio
ISBN 978-1-108-40863-9 Workbook with Audio A
ISBN 978-1-108-41192-9 Workbook with Audio B
ISBN 978-1-108-40516-4 Teacher's Edition with Test Generator
ISBN 978-1-108-41065-6 Presentation Plus
ISBN 978-1-108-41202-5 Class Audio CDs
ISBN 978-1-108-40788-5 Video Resource Book with DVD
ISBN 978-1-108-41446-3 Full Contact with DVD
ISBN 978-1-108-41153-0 Full Contact with DVD A
ISBN 978-1-108-41412-8 Full Contact with DVD B

Additional resources for this publication at www.cambridge.org/evolve

CONTENTS

UNIT 1   CONNECTIONS

1.1   WE'RE FAMILY

1   VOCABULARY: Describing people you know

A   Write the connection you have with each person: **FAM (Family), FR (Friend or Romantic), W/S (Work or School).**

1	____FR____	boyfriend
2	_____	boss
3	_____	brother
4	_____	classmate
5	_____	close friend
6	_____	girlfriend
7	_____	grandchild
8	_____	grandfather
9	_____	neighbor
10	_____	roommate

B   Where possible, write the name of a person you know next to each connection in exercise A.

2   GRAMMAR: *be*; possessive adjectives

A   Complete the text with the correct form of the verb *be*.

My name ¹____is____ Raul, and I ²_____ from Mexico.
I'm an English teacher now in Miami, Florida. These ³_____
the people in my life. My grandparents ⁴_____ Monica and
Roberto – that's them in the photo. This is their house in Valle de Bravo,
Mexico. My brothers' names ⁵_____ Sergio and Raymundo.
We ⁶_____ very close friends. This ⁷_____
a photo of me with Marisela. People always ask, ⁸"_____
she your girlfriend?" No, she ⁹_____ not!
She ¹⁰_____ my neighbor.

Match the columns.

1	I	a	_____	their
2	you	b	_____	his
3	he	c	_____	our
4	she	d	_____	her
5	it	e	_____	your
6	we	f	_1_	my
7	they	g	_____	its

3   GRAMMAR AND VOCABULARY

A   **Complete the questions for a social media profile. Then answer the questions.**

1 What _____ is _____ your name?

_____

2 Where _____ you from?

_____

3 What _____ your classmates' names?

_____

4 _____ they your friends?

_____

5 What _____ your close friend's name?

_____

6 _____ he or she your roommate?

_____

7 What _____ your boyfriend or girlfriend's name?

_____

8 _____ she or he from Canada?

_____

B   **Complete the sentences with the correct possessive adjective.**

his	her	its	~~my~~	our	their	your

1 I have a pen. This is _____ my _____ pen.
2 My boyfriend has a new car. This is _____ new car.
3 Is this _____ girlfriend? Are you close friends?
4 Marie lives near my family. She is _____ neighbor.
5 Carol and Sissy are my roommates. That is _____ room.
6 The dog is hungry. This is _____ food.
7 She is the new boss. _____ name is Ms. Singh.

WHAT'S IN YOUR BAG?

1 VOCABULARY: Naming everyday things

A **Write the words in the correct column. What things can you put in your pocket? What things can't you put in your pocket?**

| candy bar | cash | driver's license | gum | hairbrush | hand lotion |
| keychain | mirror | receipt | ~~tissues~~ | umbrella | water bottle |

In my pocket	Not in my pocket
tissues	

2 GRAMMAR: Possession

A **Circle the correct words to complete the conversation.**

Teacher Excuse me, class. *Who's / (Whose)* jacket is this?

Girl It isn't *mine / ours*. *My / Your* jacket has pockets.

Teacher Tyler, is this *yours / whose*?

Boy No. It isn't *mine / his*. *Mine / My* jacket is green.

Teacher Oh, look! Here's a name in the jacket. It belongs to Sarah. It's *hers / his*.

Boy Sarah, it's *her / your* jacket.

Sarah No, it isn't. It belongs to a different Sarah. *Mine / Yours* is blue.

B **Circle the words that are not correct in the conversation. Then correct the mistakes.**

Man Excuse me. I think that's *(mine)* wife's keychain. _____

Woman No, sorry, it isn't her. _____

Man Are you sure? I think it belong to her. _____

Woman No, it's mine. It belongs me. _____

Man Oh, I see. You're right. So where's his wife's keychain? _____

Woman Look! There's another keychain on the desk. Is that his? _____

Man No, that isn't her. _____

3 GRAMMAR AND VOCABULARY

A Circle the correct answer to complete the questions.

1 _____ mirror is that?

   a Whose   **b** Who   **c** Where

2 _____ that umbrella yours?

   a Is   **b** Are   **c** Whose

3 Whose cash _____ that?

   a are   **b** am   **c** is

4 _____ those tissues yours?

   a Is   **b** Are   **c** Whose

5 _____ candy bar is that?

   a Who   **b** Where   **c** Whose

6 _____ driver's license is that?

   a Whose   **b** Who's   **c** What

7 Does that gum _____ him?

   a belongs to   **b** belong to   **c** belong

8 Is that keychain _____?

   a our   **b** our's   **c** ours

B Answer the questions in exercise A based on the diagram below.

1 *That mirror is ours. / That's our mirror.*   5 _____

2 _____   6 _____

3 _____   7 _____

4 _____   8 _____

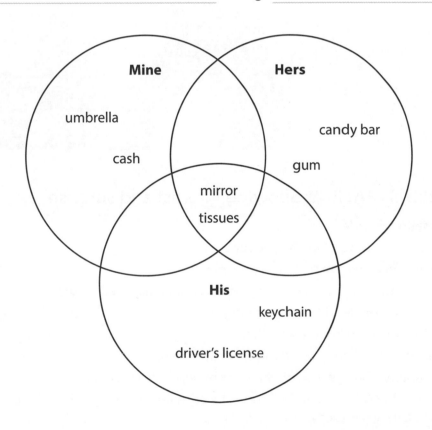

HOW DO YOU KNOW RAQUEL?

1 FUNCTIONAL LANGUAGE: Greeting someone and starting conversations

A **Complete the conversation with the phrases in the box.**

~~Are you~~	Great to meet you, too	Great to see you again
It's really good to see you	Long time, no see	Pleased to meet you

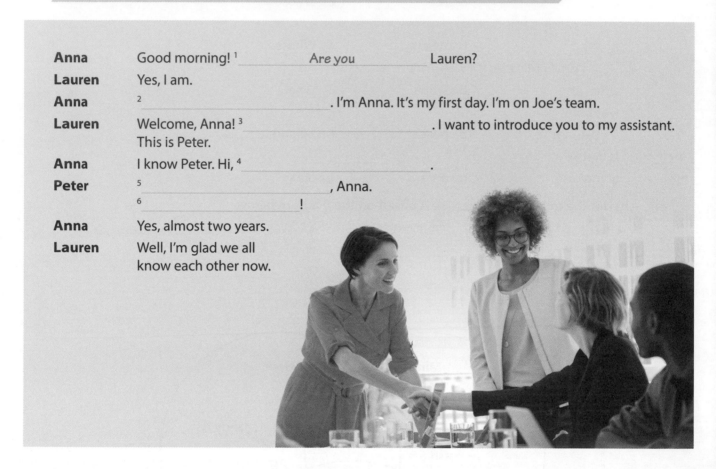

Anna	Good morning! [1]_____Are you_____ Lauren?
Lauren	Yes, I am.
Anna	[2]_____. I'm Anna. It's my first day. I'm on Joe's team.
Lauren	Welcome, Anna! [3]_____. I want to introduce you to my assistant. This is Peter.
Anna	I know Peter. Hi, [4]_____.
Peter	[5]_____, Anna.
	[6]_____!
Anna	Yes, almost two years.
Lauren	Well, I'm glad we all know each other now.

2 REAL-WORLD STRATEGY: Showing interest and surprise

A **Put the conversation in order.**

☐	**George**	Wow! Hey, Neil! Long time, no see!
1	**Neil**	Good morning. I'm Neil. Are you James?
☐	**Neil**	Yes, I know George from a long time ago. It's really great to see you.
☐	**James**	Yes, I am. Hi, Neil. Pleased to meet you.
☐	**James**	Wait … do you know each other?
☐	**Neil**	Great to meet you, too. It's my first day in sales.
☐	**James**	Seriously? George is an old friend of mine, too. This is great!
☐	**James**	Is it really? OK. Well, this is George, he's a manager. George, this is Neil, he's a new salesperson.

A **Complete the conversation with your own information.**

Carlos	I'm Carlos. Pleased to meet you.
Me	Hi, I'm ¹_____. Great ²_____.
Carlos	I recognize you from English class. It's ³_____.
Me	⁴_____? Oh, yeah, I remember you, too. Is this your first time in this class?
Carlos	Yes, it is.
Me	Great! This is my friend, ⁵_____. ⁶_____, this is Carlos.
⁷_____	Hi, Carlos. ⁸_____.
Carlos	Hey, ⁹_____. ¹⁰_____, too.
Me	Wait … do you know each other?
Carlos	Yes, we take other classes together.
Me	¹¹_____? That's awesome!

1 READING

A **Read the email and label the parts.**

Reason for writing: R   Greeting: G

End of mail: E   Closing: C

Full name: F   Introduction: I

Subject: S

Reply   Forward   ✉

_S_   **Re: Cars**

_____   Dear Thomas,

_____   My name is Anton Taft. Your cousin, Sarah Griffin, is my friend.

_____   Do you like old cars? I repair them! It's my hobby. I have a car from 1958. Attached is a photo.

_____   Please call me at 202-555-4646. We can meet on Saturday and you can see the car.

_____   Thanks!

_____   Anton Taft

---

2 LISTENING

A 🔊 **1.01** **LISTEN FOR DETAIL** **Listen to the voicemail message. Number the sentences in the order you hear them.**

☐ I want to give you some information about the summer schedule. All departments follow the new schedule starting next week. The summer schedule is in this morning's email.

☐ My name is Cindy Clark, head of the human resources department.

☐ Hello, Mr. Chen,

☐ Let me know if there are any questions.

☐ Thank you!

WRITING

A **Put the parts of the email in the correct order.**

- [ ] I want to invite you to our first neighbors' meeting. Please find the agenda for the meeting included with this letter. The meeting is at my house.
- [ ] Rick Lock
- [ ] Dear Mrs. Albertson,
- [ ] My name is Rick Lock. I'm a neighbor of yours. Welcome to the neighborhood.
- [ ] Sincerely,
- [ ] Thank you very much for your time. I look forward to seeing you at the meeting.
- [ ] Re: Upcoming meeting

B **Complete the email with your own ideas.**

> Reply   Forward
>
> **Re:** New weekend classes
>
> ¹_____ Mick,
>
> I'm Roger from the gym. ²_____?
> I hope everything is great for you!
>
> I want to invite you to my special dance classes on Saturdays and Sundays. We are starting
> ³_____. Please see the calendar included with this email.
>
> I hope ⁴_____ us.
>
> ⁵_____,
>
> Roger Strong

CHECK AND REVIEW

Read the statements. Can you do these things?

UNIT 1	Mark the boxes. ☑ I can do it. ？ I am not sure. I can …	If you are not sure, go back to these pages in the Student's Book.
VOCABULARY	☐ talk about people I know.	page 2
	☐ name everyday things.	page 4
GRAMMAR	☐ use *be*.	page 3
	☐ use possessive adjectives.	page 5
FUNCTIONAL LANGUAGE	☐ greet people and start a conversation.	page 6
	☐ show interest and surprise.	page 7
SKILLS	☐ introduce myself in an email.	page 9
	☐ use capital letters.	page 9

WORK AND STUDY

KNOW YOUR NUMBERS

1 VOCABULARY: Expressions with *do, have,* and *make*

A **Complete the actions with *do, have,* or *make*.**

_____have_____	a party	_____	a snack
_____	free time	_____	housework
_____	plans	_____	something to drink
_____	some work	_____	the bed
_____	the dishes	_____	the laundry

B **Write the phrases in exercise A in the correct column. Are there phrases that go in both columns?**

Tasks	Fun

2 GRAMMAR: Simple present for habits and routines

A **Complete the sentences with the correct form of the verbs in parentheses.**

1 I _____*don't have*_____ (not have) much free time tomorrow.

2 We always _____ (have) a party for my birthday.

3 _____ they _____ (do sleep) for eight hours every night? No, they _____ (do).

4 He usually _____ (have) something to drink with dinner.

5 She _____ (do) the dishes and then _____ (have) a snack every day.

6 Sam _____ (not make) plans for after work.

7 My roommate _____ (not make) his bed but he _____ (do) the laundry every week.

8 Ben _____ (usually do) the housework. I _____ (not do) the housework, but I _____ (always do) the laundry.

B **Correct the sentences.**

1 They often in the afternoon do the dishes.

They often do the dishes in the afternoon.

2 I don't on Mondays do the laundry.

3 Julia makes plans with her mom at night sometimes.

4 Peter and I have something to drink often with dinner.

5 When do you have free time usually?

6 How does he do housework often?

7 Every morning I do some work on my computer.

8 We have a snack never before dinner.

3 GRAMMAR AND VOCABULARY

A **Write the names of the people in your home who do the following actions. Then write when they do it.**

do the dishes	do housework	do the laundry
have a snack	make plans	make the bed

What	Who	When
do the dishes	_my ..._	_every ..._

B **Write sentences using the information in exercise A.**

1 _My sister usually does the dishes every Saturday._

2

3

4

5

6

WHERE'S YOUR WORKSPACE?

1 VOCABULARY: Naming work and study items

A **Cross out the word that is different.**

1 mouse	~~textbook~~	Wi-Fi	keyboard
2 document	files	note	outlet
3 keyboard	calendar	computer	mouse
4 home	office	school	document
5 files	calendar	textbook	headphones
6 calendar	keyboard	files	document

B **Label the pictures below with words in exercise A.**

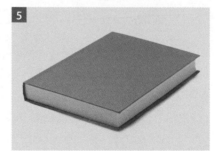

2 GRAMMAR: *This / that one*; *these / those ones*

A **Circle the correct words to complete the sentences.**

1 I like to clean my office every week. You see all *these* / *those* papers here on my desk? They are documents that I usually keep in *that / this* cabinet over there. But I'm working on many jobs now, so I have all of them here for the moment.

2 I share this office with Tim. He likes to listen to music. *Those ones / Those* are his headphones on his chair. I usually sit by the window. I watch people buy their newspapers at *that / this* newsstand on the corner.

3 We have many laptops in our office. *This one / This* is my favorite. I like it because the keyboard is big. It has a wider screen than *these / those* by the door. I usually use it.

B   Ask the people in the pictures about the objects. Complete your questions and their answers. Use *this,*
    that, these, or *those,* and *this / that one* or *these / those ones.*

1 **A** What is _____?
   B _____ is my table.
2 **A** Is _____ your favorite umbrella?
   B Yes, it's _____ _____.
3 **A** What are _____?
   B _____ are Tim and Laura's chairs.
4 **A** _____ desk is where I usually work.
   B It's bigger than _____ over there.

3 GRAMMAR AND VOCABULARY

A   Look at the picture. Circle the correct answers about the things in the picture.

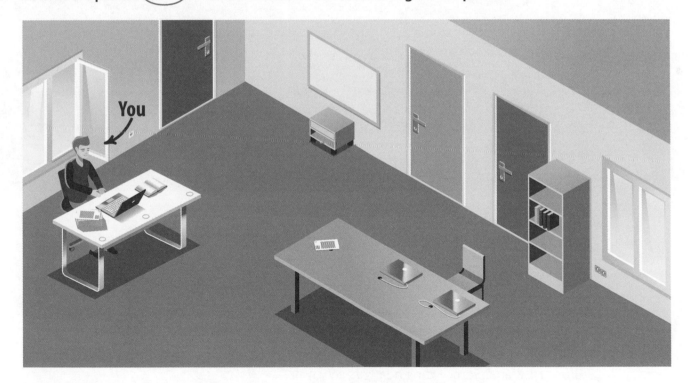

1 *This is / These are* an open laptop. *That one / Those ones* aren't open.
2 *This / These* documents *is / are* on the desk. *That one / Those ones is / are* on the table.
3 *This is / These are* a modern desk. *That is / Those are* a table.
4 *This is / These are* an open window. *That one isn't / Those ones aren't* open.

B   Choose other things in the picture. Write sentences like the ones in exercise A
    using *this / that one* and *these / those.*

    _____   _____

    _____   _____

THE CONNECTION'S TERRIBLE

1 FUNCTIONAL LANGUAGE: Explaining communication problems

A **Put the conversation in order.**

|1| **Maria** Hi, Julio. How are you?

|☐| **Maria** OK … How about now? Julio? Are you still there?

|☐| **Maria** Hm … I think it's my Wi-Fi. Let me see … Is that any better?

|☐| **Maria** Hm … Let me call you again, OK?

|☐| **Maria** I can't. I have meetings all day. Let me change my mic … How about now?

|☐| **Julio** Uh, … It's not better, sorry. The echo is still there.

|☐| **Julio** Hi. Maria? Sorry, I can't hear you very well.

|☐| **Julio** No, I'm sorry. Maria, you're breaking up. The connection is terrible

|☐| **Julio** Yes, I'm still here, but there's an echo now. Can we try again later today?

|☐| **Julio** OK. Thanks.

2 REAL-WORLD STRATEGY: Asking for repetition and confirmation

A Match the columns to complete the questions.

1 Sorry, I …   a _____ any better?
2 Can you …   b _____ hear me OK?
3 Are you …   c _____ about now?
4 Sorry, can …   d _____ didn't catch that.
5 How …   e _____ still there?
6 Is that …   f _____ you say that again?

3 FUNCTIONAL LANGUAGE AND REAL-WORLD STRATEGY

A Write a phone conversation that describes a problem with a bad phone connection. Before you write the conversation, complete the chart with the situation and the expressions you plan to use.

Situation	
Explaining the problem	
Checking the problem	
Solving the problem	
Asking for repetition	

B Write the conversation using the expressions in exercise A.

A Hi. _____

B _____

A _____

B _____

A _____

B _____

A _____

B _____

HOW TO BE SUCCESSFUL

1 LISTENING

A 🔊 **2.01** **Listen to the podcast. (Circle) the correct answers.**

1 What does Ada do after breakfast?

   a She calls clients.   **b** She writes stories.   **c** She uses her computer.

2 Why does she like her workspace?

   a It has a big table.   **b** She can make lots of coffee.

   c There is a lot of light.

3 How does she work?

   a on her laptop   **b** on her tablet   **c** with pen and paper

4 What is the interview about?

   a being successful   **b** daily habits   **c** fame and fortune

B 🔊 **2.01** **LISTEN FOR DETAIL** **Listen to the podcast again. Match the columns to complete the sentences.**

1 Ada usually _____   **a** after she writes down her ideas.

2 The room where she works _____   **b** plans a new book.

3 She writes new notes _____   **c** writes more than 1,000 words a day.

4 She never _____   **d** is her favorite place in the house.

5 She uses her computer _____   **e** on paper.

2 READING

A **Read the magazine article. (Circle) the correct answers to complete the sentences.**

Lessons In Life

Damian Brand offers four lessons to help you with your career choices.

There is a famous quotation by American inventor and businessman Thomas Alva Edison (1847–1931): "Genius is 1% inspiration and 99% perspiration." So, lesson number one: if you want something in life, you need to work really hard for it.

Lesson in life number two: do what you love. If your job is about something you really like, you have a very good start. I believe that people who work hard are people who usually love their jobs.

Lesson number three: know what you want to achieve and how you can achieve it. My advice is to make a list of goals and practical things you can do to achieve them.

Lesson four: believe in your talents, and don't give up. It's easy to think that employers don't want you or what you can do. But your big break is just around the corner …

1 This article says that success is *easy / hard* work.

2 It helps if you *enjoy / don't like* what you do.

3 Goals *help / invite* you to be successful.

4 Don't stop *working / playing*.

B Read the article again. (Circle) the correct answers.

1 What does Thomas Edison's quotation mean? It means it's important to …

   a have talent.   **b** work hard.   **c** have talent and work hard.

2 Why does Damian think that people work hard? Because they …

   a don't have a choice.   **b** love their jobs.   **c** make a lot of money.

3 What is Damian's advice about career goals?

   a Have goals you can achieve.   **b** Make a list of jobs you want.   **c** Have big dreams.

3 WRITING

A Read the following statements. Give your opinion about them using the phrases in the box.

another example	for example	I don't believe	like all others	very interesting

1 All famous businesspeople are successful.

   I don't believe all famous businesspeople are successful. For example …

2 All successful people are very organized.

3 Successful people play sports and have interesting habits.

4 You need to earn a lot of money to become successful.

5 Success is about having a lot of people work for you.

B Write a blog entry about your daily habits and how you think they help you become a successful person. Include as many examples as possible.

CHECK AND REVIEW

Read the statements. Can you do these things?

UNIT 2	Mark the boxes. ☑ I can do it. ☐? I am not sure. I can …	If you are not sure, go back to these pages in the Student's Book.
VOCABULARY	☐ use expressions with *do*, *have*, and *make*. ☐ name work and study items.	page 12 page 14
GRAMMAR	☐ use the simple present to describe habits and routines. ☐ use *this / that one*; *these / those ones* to talk about objects near and far.	page 13 page 15
FUNCTIONAL LANGUAGE	☐ talk about communication problems. ☐ ask someone to repeat something.	page 16 page 17
SKILLS	☐ write my opinion of a podcast. ☐ use correct spelling.	page 19 page 19

1 VOCABULARY: Sports

Across:

Down:

A   **Look at the pictures and complete the crossword.**

B   **Complete the sentences. Use the correct form of the words from the crossword in exercise A.**

1   Many _____fans_____ are excited to see their team play tonight.

2   The _____ is full! There are so many people exercising!

3   There is my favorite soccer _____! Hi, Cristiano!

4   Del Potro is a great Argentinian tennis player! He is _____ the set, 30–20.

5   I love tennis! Look! Serena Williams is on the _____ now!

6   Wait! There are only nine players on the soccer _____.

7   The swimmers are jumping into the _____.

8   Chile is _____ to the other _____! Argentina is going to win!

9   The Australian runners are winning the 1,600-meter _____!

2 GRAMMAR: Present continuous

A **Complete the sentences using the present continuous. Use the pictures to help you.**

1 She _____ (talk) to the man.

2 He _____ (have) a drink of water.

3 They _____ (talk) together.

4 Laverne and Marconie _____ (win).

B **Look at the pictures. What is each picture about? Write a sentence about each one.**

1 _____ **2** _____ **3** _____ **4** _____

3 GRAMMAR AND VOCABULARY

A **Complete the conversation with your own information.**

A Where are you?

B I'm ¹ _____. And guess what?
² _____ is standing right next to me!

A No way! What's ³ _____ doing?

B ⁴ _____

A Awesome!

B **Use the present continuous to write a conversation about a famous athlete you see. Use the words and phrases in the box or your own words. Look at the conversation in the right column and use it as a model.**

awesome	doing	guess what	score	take a photo	talk to a player
team	what	where	who	win	

A _____ **A** Where are you now?

B _____ **B** I'm at the airport. And guess what? The Giants baseball team is sitting here!

A _____ **A** Really? What are they doing?

B _____ **B** I think they're waiting for a plane.

A _____ **A** Awesome! That's your favorite team!

THE 16TH STEP

1 VOCABULARY: Exercising

A **Read the three interviews and complete the text. Use the correct form of the verbs in the box.**

| jump | lie down | lift | ~~sit down~~ | stretch | throw |

A Yoga is my favorite exercise. I'm waiting for my class to start. The class is very good and a lot of people take it. The teacher ¹_____*sits down*_____ in front of the class and we sit behind him. Here we are ²_____ our bodies to warm up. Then we ³_____ on the floor at the end of class. I love that part!

B My daughter is taking a dance class. She likes it because her friends from school are in the same class. The girls are ⁴_____ their arms above their heads at the moment. The teacher asks them to follow her instructions.

C My friends and I play on a baseball team. We meet every Thursday in the park. First, we ⁵_____ balls for a few minutes to warm up. We are ⁶_____ up and down in the photo because we're happy! My friends and I love this sport!

2 GRAMMAR: Simple present and present continuous

A **Write the verbs in parentheses in the correct form.**

1 Tony _____*plays*_____ (play) football every weekend.

2 We _____ (lift) our arms at the moment.

3 Sari _____ (climb) up the stairs to get to class every day.

4 They _____ (lie) down on the floor at the moment.

5 How many people _____ (swim) in the pool right now?

6 How often _____ (he / run)?

7 What kind of exercise _____ (they / do) now?

8 _____ (your boyfriend / watch) the game on TV this afternoon?

B **Correct the sentences.**

1 Are you stretching every morning when you wake up?

_____

2 Look! I lift two coffee cups now!

_____

3 I'm not going to the gym every evening.

_____

4 Look! The fans are run onto the field!

_____

5 The race is on. Everyone is run.

_____

6 Do you listening to the game on the radio now?

_____

7 Your dog lies down under the tree.

_____

8 Are all the athletes exercise at the gym now?

_____

3 GRAMMAR AND VOCABULARY

A **Complete the gym questionnaire with your own answers.**

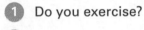

1 Do you exercise? _____

2 Are you a gym member? _____

3 Do you play a sport? _____

4 What is your regular exercise routine? _____

5 What sports do you like? _____

6 Do you prefer to exercise in the morning, afternoon, or at night? _____

3.3 COULD YOU TELL ME ... ?

1 FUNCTIONAL LANGUAGE: Asking for information

A Put the conversation in order.

- [ ] Near the exit, thanks. Oh, one more thing, could you tell me where the coffee shop is?
- [ ] It's right by the entrance.
- [1] Excuse me. We're looking for row B.
- [ ] It's three rows down.
- [ ] Thank you so much and have a great day.
- [ ] They are near the exit by center court.
- [ ] Oh, great! Thanks. Do you know where the restrooms are?

B Complete the conversation with the expressions in exercise A.

A Excuse me. I'm [1]_____ a small sun hat for a girl.

B The sun hats are over there, on the right.

A OK, thanks. Also, [2]_____ the price of these sunglasses?

B No problem. They're $16.00.

A Oh! OK, thank you.

2 REAL-WORLD STRATEGY: Checking information

A Match the sentences 1–5 with the correct responses a–e.

1 Excuse me. Do you know where the VIP seats are?

2 Could you tell me when the game starts?

3 Excuse me. I'm looking for the entrance to the gym.

4 Oh wow, the score is 3–1, Manchester United.

5 Excuse me. Where is the basketball practice?

a _____ 3–1? I can't believe it!

b _____ The entrance? It's around the corner.

c _____ Basketball practice? It's at the May Center.

d _____ The game? I think it starts at 5 p.m.

e _____ The VIP seats? They are next to the court.

FUNCTIONAL LANGUAGE AND REAL-WORLD STRATEGY

A **Complete the conversation. Use the words in parentheses.**

> **A** Excuse me. ¹_____ (look for) court number three. I have a tennis lesson.
>
> **B** Of course. The teacher ²_____ (wait / now). The court is out this door.
>
> **A** Out this door? OK. ³_____ (could / tell) the teacher's name?
>
> **B** ⁴_____? Well, it's Giuliana Silva, but we call her Ace.
>
> **A** Ace? Great! Just one more thing. ⁵_____ (know / where) I can get a towel?
>
> **B** ⁶_____ (towel)? Sure, no problem. I can get one for you. Here you go.
>
> **A** Thank you!

B **Use exercise A to write a similar conversation using the information below.**

A _____
B _____
A _____
B _____
A _____
B _____
A _____

BIKE SHARING

1 LISTENING

A 🔊 **3.01** **Listen to the radio interview about the *Bicitekas* in Mexico City. Read the sentences and write *T* if True or *F* if False. Write the correct answers.**

1 _____ Adrian's group has bicycle tours to teach people about art.

_____

2 _____ Adrian rides his bicycle to his job at the theater every day.

_____

3 _____ Adrian wears a helmet and gloves when he rides his bicycle.

_____

4 _____ Adrian's group has night tours.

_____

B 🔊 **3.01** **LISTEN FOR DETAIL** **Listen to the interview again and answer the questions.**

1 What is the name of Adrian's group? _____

2 Where is his group from? _____

3 How many people ride bicycles in Mexico City on the weekend? _____

4 When are the night tours? _____

5 How many people usually take the tours? _____

2 READING

A **Read the online article and (circle) the correct answers.**

● ● ● ⟨ ⟩   🔍 🏠

Cities for People or Cars?

Too many cars can be bad for a city. There is too much traffic and stress. And traffic can be a problem because stressed drivers sometimes break the rules to save time.

At the *Bicitekas* group, we think bicycles can help change people's habits. That is why we have bicycle tours around the city, and we plan art shows and parties. Mexico City needs better roads and more green areas.

There are many ways you can help. Come to our shows, tours, and parties. And, above all, use your bike. Do not drive your car on the weekend, and share rides with friends and family. You can help us make our city a better place for people and not just for cars.

1 What is the main idea?

  a Cars are good.   **b** People can help.   **c** The city needs more parks.

2 What does *Bicitekas* do?

  a sells bicycles   **b** has bike tours   **c** repairs old bicycles

3 What does the author say people can do to help?

  a share rides   **b** drive on weekends   **c** buy a newer car

A   **Match the sentences. Then complete them with the correct word from the box.**

> and   but   so

1   There aren't any bike docking stations at the subway station, _____

2   The local park has a bike lane, _____

3   My street needs a park, trees, _____

a   _____ they don't rent bikes to park visitors.

b   _____ more green areas.

c   _____ I have to walk home from the station.

B   **Use the sentences in exercise A, and write three comments on your neighborhood's website about the things missing in your area. Don't forget to use *and*, *but*, and *so*.**

CHECK AND REVIEW

Read the statements. Can you do these things?

UNIT 3	Mark the boxes. ☑ I can do it. ？ I am not sure. I can ...	If you are not sure, go back to these pages in the Student's Book.
VOCABULARY	☐ use sports words. ☐ use words to describe exercise.	page 22 page 25
GRAMMAR	☐ use the present continuous for events happening now. ☐ understand the difference between simple present and present continuous.	page 23 page 25
FUNCTIONAL LANGUAGE	☐ ask for information in different situations. ☐ check information.	page 26 page 27
SKILLS	☐ write a short message. ☐ use *and*, *but*, and *so*.	page 29 page 29

4.1   COMIC CELEBRATION

1   VOCABULARY: Describing pop culture

A   **Find the words from the box in the word search.**

actor	artist	band	concert
director	festival	~~musician~~	singer
TV show	video games		

```
U  U  V  T  T  T  W  K  D  E  B  G
N  V  X  Q  V  T  S  D  T  F  A  C
G  I  S  V  S  Y  I  I  T  N  N  D
P  D  H  M  H  I  N  R  S  N  D  Y
L  E  R  M  O  O  G  E  I  E  N  F
V  O  S  E  W  L  E  C  T  T  A  E
K  G  B  W  G  Y  R  T  R  D  C  S
O  A  R  T  I  S  T  O  A  X  T  T
H  M  L  W  J  V  I  R  R  N  O  I
L  E  I  H  P  R  V  S  T  E  R  V
D  S  H  X  C  O  N  C  E  R  T  A
T  N (M  U  S  I  C  I  A  N) P  L
```

2   GRAMMAR: Present continuous for future plans

A   **Label each sentence *F* for future or *P* for present.**

1 I'm going to a theater festival this weekend.   F

2 My friend's band is playing tonight at Red Note.   _____

3 She's in her room. I think she's watching a TV show. _____

4 Are you doing anything tonight?   _____

5 I'm getting a new video game tomorrow.   _____

6 What are you listening to? Can I listen?   _____

B **Put the conversation in order.**

☐ I love them! What time are you leaving?

☐ Not really. I'm playing video games now, but that's all. How about you?

☐ In an hour. So, are you coming?

☐ Oh, yeah! I'm coming with you.

☐ I'm going to a music festival. A friend of mine is playing in a band.

☐ It's called Public Attack. The Bronxites and Sam and the Wheelers are also playing.

☐ That's great! What's the name of his band? Are other bands playing, too?

1 Are you doing anything tonight?

3 GRAMMAR AND VOCABULARY

A **Complete the chart with your own plans.**

Who	What	When
Anna	watch a movie	this weekend
Jose	go to a concert	tonight
Anna and Jose	play video games	tomorrow
I	_____	tomorrow
I	_____	this weekend
A friend and I	_____	next week

B **Write sentences using the information in exercise A.**

1 Anna is watching a movie this weekend.

2 _____

3 _____

4 _____

5 _____

6 _____

4.2 THE PERFECT GIFT

1 VOCABULARY: Naming gift items

A **Read the sentence about each person and then choose the best gift.**

1 Alex often works in her garden.
   a a bouquet of flowers
   b a phone charger
   c a candle

2 Jose loves his laptop.
   a candy
   b perfume
   c speakers

3 Marta always wears earrings.
   a a purse
   b jewelry
   c a phone charger

4 Jonathan always wears comfortable clothes.
   a a candle
   b a sweatshirt
   c speakers

5 Sari often eats desserts.
   a candy
   b a candle
   c perfume

6 It's really difficult to buy gifts for Tony.
   a a phone charger
   b a candle
   c a gift card

2 GRAMMAR: Object pronouns

A **Complete the sentences using the words in the box.**

| ~~her~~ | him | it | me | them | us | you |

1 I always give my mom a bouquet of flowers. It's the best gift for _____ her _____.
2 Sometimes I buy candy for my brother. It makes _____ happy!
3 Tomorrow is your birthday! I'm giving _____ speakers for your laptop.
4 My brothers, sisters, and I are going to my grandparents' house on Sunday.
   They often invite _____ for a family dinner.
5 I have a candle for you! I hope you like _____!
6 My friends know what I like. They always buy great gifts for _____!
7 I'm getting new pants for my sister. I'm buying _____ tomorrow.

B **Rewrite the sentences using object pronouns.**

1 Donald is a Yankees' baseball fan. He watches **the Yankees** play every weekend.

   Donald is a Yankees' baseball fan. He watches them play every weekend.

2 I'm buying a new camera for you. I hope you like **the new camera**.

_____

3 Those are beautiful flowers! Do you like **the flowers**?

_____

4 My dad always gives me good advice. I love **my dad**!

_____

5 Jack, Katie, and I are going to Comic Con. I'm glad you're coming with **Jack, Katie, and me**.

_____

6 It's my sister's birthday. She has so many hobbies, I don't know what to give **my sister**.

_____

3 GRAMMAR AND VOCABULARY

A **Complete the conversation with your own information.**

A I want to give my [1]_____ a birthday gift, but I don't know what to get [2]_____.

B OK, well. What does [3]_____ like to do? What are [4]_____ hobbies?

A I'm not sure. I think [5]_____ likes [6]_____.

B OK. How about [7]_____? Do you think [8]_____ might like [9]_____?

A That's a great idea! Thanks for helping [10]_____!

B Sure! That's what friends are for!

4.3 I'D LOVE TO!

FUNCTIONAL LANGUAGE: Making and responding to invitations; making plans to meet

A **Match the columns to complete the conversations.**

1 Would you like to come to the concert tonight?
2 We can meet you at seven at the theater.
3 Let's meet in front of the bus station.
4 Hey, Ray! What's up?
5 We're meeting at the entrance to the park.

a _____ Great! See you there!
b _____ Not much. How about you?
c _____ OK, let's meet there at seven.
d _____ OK. Where is the station from here?
e _____ Sorry, I can't. I'm busy tonight.

2 **REAL-WORLD STRATEGY:** Giving general excuses

A **Complete the chart with sentences from the conversation.**

1 **A** Hi, Lauren. Mark and I are going dancing. Would you like to come?
2 **B** I'm not sure. I have homework and everything.
3 **A** Come with us! We can leave in two hours. Can you finish your homework in two hours?
4 **B** I think I can. OK, I'd love to.
5 **A** Great! We can meet at my place in two hours. We're getting a taxi from there.
6 **B** OK. See you there!

Purpose	Number of line
Decide on a time and a place to meet	_____
Say yes to the invitation	_____
Say no and give a general excuse	_____
Invite someone to do something with you	1
Agree on your new plans	_____
Explain more about the plans	_____

FUNCTIONAL LANGUAGE AND REAL-WORLD STRATEGY

A **Look at the pictures and choose one event. You will write a conversation planning to meet with friends at this event.**

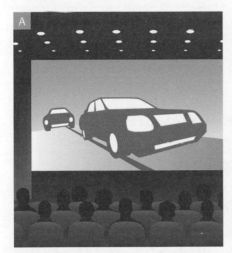

B **Before you write the conversation, complete the chart with expressions you plan to use.**

Purpose	Expressions
Ask how people are	What's up?
Ask about their plans	What are you doing …?
Invite someone to do something with you	
Give a general excuse	
Explain more about the plans	
Accept the invitation	
Decide on a time and a place to meet	
Agree on your new plans	

C **Write your conversation with the expressions from exercise B.**

A Hey. _____?

B _____

A _____

B _____

A _____

B _____

A _____

B _____

A _____

1 LISTENING

A   🔊 4.01   **Listen to the podcast.** (Circle) **the correct answers.**

1 What is the name of the festival?

   a   The Black Rock City Festival   **b**   Burning Man   **c**   The Nevada Festival

2 What is the festival famous for?

   a   its people   **b**   its fans   **c**   its art

3 How long does it last?

   a   a year   **b**   a week   **c**   a month

4 The festival happens in _____ .

   a   the city   **b**   the jungle   **c**   the desert

B   🔊 4.01   **LISTEN FOR DETAIL**   **Listen to the podcast again. Match the phrases to complete the sentences.**

1 This year about 70,000 people …   **a** _____ help you find the artist in you.

2 It is a time for them …   **b** _____ TV shows talk about it.

3 They say it can …   **c** _____ for a whole week.

4 People live in the desert …   **d** _____ are coming to Nevada.

5 It is so popular that …   **e** _____ to meet other people.

6 This is the thirty-third year …   **f** _____ of the festival.

2 READING

A   **Read the blog post and** (circle) **the correct answers.**

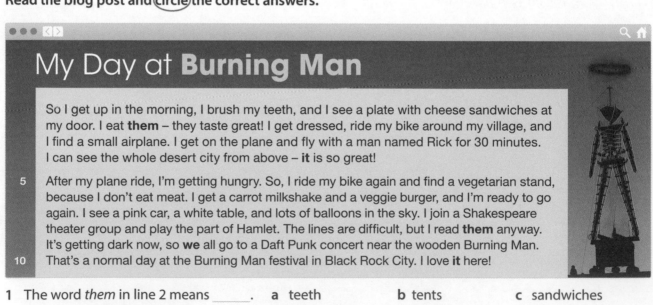

My Day at **Burning Man**

So I get up in the morning, I brush my teeth, and I see a plate with cheese sandwiches at my door. I eat **them** – they taste great! I get dressed, ride my bike around my village, and I find a small airplane. I get on the plane and fly with a man named Rick for 30 minutes. I can see the whole desert city from above – **it** is so great!

5   After my plane ride, I'm getting hungry. So, I ride my bike again and find a vegetarian stand, because I don't eat meat. I get a carrot milkshake and a veggie burger, and I'm ready to go again. I see a pink car, a white table, and lots of balloons in the sky. I join a Shakespeare theater group and play the part of Hamlet. The lines are difficult, but I read **them** anyway. It's getting dark now, so **we** all go to a Daft Punk concert near the wooden Burning Man.

10   That's a normal day at the Burning Man festival in Black Rock City. I love **it** here!

1 The word *them* in line 2 means _____ .   **a** teeth   **b** tents   **c** sandwiches

2 The word *it* in line 4 means _____ .   **a** an airplane   **b** a bike   **c** a city

3 The word *them* in line 8 means _____ .   **a** a theater group   **b** lines in a play   **c** balloons

4 The word *we* in line 9 means _____ .   **a** the band   **b** a theater group   **c** Rick and his friends

5 The word *it* in line 10 means _____ .   **a** a wooden man   **b** a festival   **c** a concert

A   🔊 4.01   Listen to the podcast again and read the information below. Write an email and invite your friend to the Burning Man festival. Use the information below to write your invitation. Check your spelling.

DATE: August 27 – September 4
PRICE: $425.00
EVENTS: Theater groups, Fire circles, Music concerts, Art competition
PLACE: Black Rock City in the Nevada desert

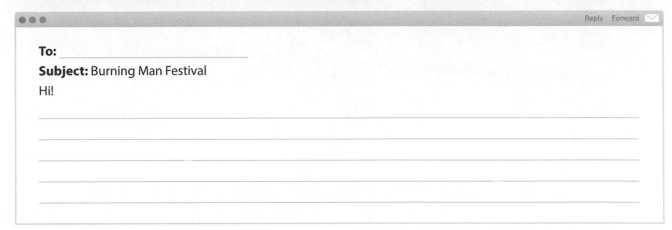

Reply   Forward

To: _____
Subject: Burning Man Festival
Hi!

CHECK AND REVIEW

Read the statements. Can you do these things?

UNIT 4	Mark the boxes. ☑ I can do it. ? I am not sure.		If you are not sure, go back to these pages in the Student's Book.
	I can …		
VOCABULARY	☐ use words to talk about pop culture.		page 34
	☐ use words to talk about gifts.		page 36
GRAMMAR	☐ use the present continuous to talk about future plans.		page 35
	☐ use object pronouns.		page 37
FUNCTIONAL LANGUAGE	☐ make and respond to invitations.		page 38
	☐ make plans to meet.		page 38
	☐ use general language to give excuses.		page 39
SKILLS	☐ write an online invitation.		page 41

5.1 ONE AMAZING DAY

1 VOCABULARY: Describing opinions and feelings

A **Look at the emojis and label them using the words in the box.**

amazing	angry	cool	crazy	~~dangerous~~	fun
horrible	loud	perfect	proud	strange	tired

1 _____ 5 _____ 9 _____

2 _____ 6 _____ 10 _____

3 _____ 7 _dangerous_____ 11 _____

4 _____ 8 _____ 12 _____

2 GRAMMAR: Simple past

A **Read the clues and complete the crossword with the past form of the verbs in bold.**

Across:

2 They **are** my friends.

3 I **have** a lot of work to do.

6 It **is** my birthday.

7 I **study** for my test in the library.

8 What **do** you do for fun?

Down:

1 I **learn** new things in art class.

2 Tim **walks** five miles to school.

4 I often **visit** the aquarium in Boston.

5 The cat **rests** in the sun all afternoon.

6 I **go** to work early in the morning.

B Rewrite the sentences using the past form of the verbs and the words in parentheses.

1 I see my friends at school every day. (yesterday)

_____

2 They visit their grandparents every year. (last year)

_____

3 Is he your best friend? (in elementary school)

_____

4 Sam has dinner plans with her classmates. (last night)

_____

5 Are the Patriots the winners this season? (last season)

_____

3   GRAMMAR AND VOCABULARY

A **Write three short stories about your past that were:**

Amazing: _____

_____

_____

Dangerous: _____

_____

_____

Strange: _____

_____

_____

B **Choose two stories from exercise A and answer the following questions about them.**

Questions	First story	Second story
Was this good or bad for you?		
Who were you with?		
Why was this moment special?		

1   VOCABULARY: Describing life events

A   Write each action under the correct life stage.

be born	become a grandparent	buy a car
~~buy a house or apartment~~	get a job	get married
graduate from college	have a baby	learn to drive
meet your future husband/wife	retire	start school

Children and youth	Adults	Old age
	buy a house or apartment	

2   GRAMMAR: Simple past negative and questions

A   Put the words in the correct order to make sentences.

1   move / Mia / When / to / did / Rio de Janeiro?

   When did Mia move to Rio de Janeiro?

2   did / go / Mia / school / to / Where?

   _____

3   brother's / her / name / was / What?

   _____

4   meet / her / she / husband / did / Where?

   _____

5   and her husband / children / did / have / How many / Mia?

   _____

6   children / didn't / have / They / three.

   _____

7   her / job / was / What?

   _____

8   did / How long / she / there / work?

   _____

9   Did / her / job / like / she?

   _____

10   Did / her / his / husband / job / like?

   _____

B Complete the interview about a famous Brazilian soccer player, Pelé. Use the past forms of the words in the box. Some words will be used more than once.

be	become	do	help
(not) be	play	score	

When ¹_____was_____ Pelé born?

He was born on October 23, 1940.

Where ²_____ he born?

In Três Corações, Brazil.

What ³_____ his life like?

Pelé ⁴_____ rich when he was born. He grew up very poor, but he was always a great soccer player. He ⁵_____ a professional soccer player when he ⁶_____ 15 years old. One year later, he ⁷_____ more goals than any other player and ⁸_____ for Brazil's national team.

When ⁹_____ he become a superstar?

At the 1958 World Cup in Sweden. At 17 years old, he ¹⁰_____ three goals in the semifinal against France, and ¹¹_____ the Brazilian team become the world's best team when they scored two more goals in the final game against Sweden.

3 GRAMMAR AND VOCABULARY

A **Look at Pelé's personal fact file and write sentences about him.**

First marriage	Rosemeri dos Reis Cholbi, February 21, 1966
First baby	Kelly Cristina, January 1967
First grandchild	August 1987
College	No
First World Cup	1958, 17 years old
Last World Cup	Mexico 1970
Retirement	1977
FIFA Ballon d'Or Prix d'Honneur	January 2014

Personal life

Pelé married Rosemeri dos Reis Cholbi on February 21, 1966.

_____

_____

World Cup victories

_____

_____

Age when he retired, and what he did after that

_____

_____

5.3 THAT'S COOL!

1 FUNCTIONAL LANGUAGE: Congratulating and sympathizing with people

A **Circle the best expression to complete the conversations.**

1 You got the job!

    a You did really well!   **b** Congratulations!   **c** Never mind.

2 I passed the test.

    a I'm so sorry!   **b** Never mind.   **c** That's great news!

3 She lost her keys.

    a I'm so sorry.   **b** Congratulations!   **c** That's great news!

4 She spent ten hours in the airport.

    a Never mind.   **b** That's terrible. Talk about bad luck.   **c** Don't worry about it.

5 I forgot your books.

    a Great job!   **b** That's terrible. Talk about bad luck.   **c** Don't worry about it.

2 REAL-WORLD STRATEGY: Checking your understanding

A **Match each statement to the best response.**

1 I thought you said his house was near.

2 We have a new member of the family!

3 I'm a writer!

4 I'm disappointed!

5 So you mean it's not safe to swim in the ocean?

a _____ You mean you published your novel?

b _____ So you mean you didn't win first prize?

c _____ I meant it's not safe now, but maybe you can swim later.

d ___1___ I meant it's near my house, not yours.

e _____ Do you mean you had a baby?

A **Complete the conversation with the best expressions.**

A I heard you got married last month! [1]_____!

B We did! Thanks! It was a really big decision.

A [2]_____ it was a life decision?

B Yes! I'm really happy about it! We went to Rio after the wedding.

A [3]_____!

B I know! Jim and I were really busy the month before!

A I'm sure you were. [4]_____!

B Thanks!

B **Look at the picture. Write a conversation between the two friends using the correct sympathy expressions. Use the conversation in exercise A as a model.**

A Hey, I heard you had an accident.

B [1]_____.

A [2]_____ Did you get hurt?

B Yes, well, I went to the hospital. But I'm OK now.

A [3]_____.

B Thanks! [4]_____.

1 LISTENING

A 🔊 **5.01** LISTEN FOR DETAIL **Listen to the story and (circle) the correct answers. Then listen again to check your answers.**

1 Why did Philippe want to go to the Caribbean?

  a He wanted to teach French.

  b He never visited before.

  c He wanted to see his family.

2 Where is Claire from?

  a Anse Noire   **b** Bogotá   **c** Martinique

3 How did Claire feel after going fishing?

  a excited   **b** proud   **c** perfect

4 What problem did Claire have on her vacation?

  a She didn't speak French.   **b** She didn't like the food.   **c** She didn't know anyone there.

5 What does Claire want to do before she returns to Martinique?

  a take swimming lessons   **b** learn to cook   **c** study French

2 READING

A READING FOR MAIN IDEAS **Read the text. Then (circle) the correct words to complete the sentences.**

My first time in Buenos Aires was amazing and strange at the same time. I'm from a small town in Oklahoma, so I like quiet and food – lots of food. And I had lots of great meals in Buenos Aires, especially the meat.

Everything was great for the first two days, but it changed on the third day. This happened when the town's soccer team, *River Plate*, won the *Libertadores* Cup for the fifth time.

That evening, soccer fans partied all night in the streets. There was loud music and dancing everywhere! I was not able to sleep! I don't understand why people do that when their team wins.

All this taught me a lesson. I love Buenos Aires – the people, the food – I even love Argentinian soccer! So, I want to go back, but not during any big soccer games. That I'm sure of.

1 The text is about *soccer fans in / a trip to* Buenos Aires.

2 The writer *liked / didn't like* Argentinian food.

3 The writer enjoyed *all of his time / part of his time* in Buenos Aires.

4 He learned never to travel to Argentina *again / during soccer games*.

B **Read the text again and answer the questions below.**

1 What's the name of the Buenos Aires soccer team? _____

2 Where in the US is the writer from? _____

3 What food did he eat a lot in Buenos Aires? _____

4 Does the writer love Argentinian soccer? _____

5 Is he ever going back to Buenos Aires? _____

WRITING

A **Read the conversations. Complete them with the phrases in the box. Some phrases can be used more than once.**

> Absolutely!   Are you kidding?   I know the feeling.   Interesting!
> No way!   You're so right.

1 **A** I had a great time in Seattle! What about you?

  B _____Absolutely!_____ We had so much fun there!

2 **A** Was it difficult for you to order food in Bogotá?

  B _____ We ate anything we wanted, and people in the restaurants were always friendly.

3 **A** When I got to Berlin, I didn't understand German at all!

  B _____ I was there last year, and the same thing happened to me.

4 **A** Wow. There were a lot of police officers in American airports!

  B _____ I had the same experience.

5 **A** Paris is a very unfriendly place!

  B _____ I think it's a very friendly city.

6 **A** People in Hawaii traditionally say "Aloha" and give you a beautiful flower when you first arrive.

  B _____

7 **A** I was so tired when I arrived in Sydney.

  B _____ I slept for ten hours when I went to Hong Kong.

8 **A** Do you want to live and work in another country?

  B _____ I love living here!

CHECK AND REVIEW

Read the statements. Can you do these things?

UNIT 5	Mark the boxes. ☑ I can do it. ？ I am not sure. I can …	If you are not sure, go back to these pages in the Student's Book.
VOCABULARY	☐ use adjectives to describe opinions and feelings.	page 44
	☐ use words to describe life events.	page 46
GRAMMAR	☐ use the simple past to talk about past experiences.	page 45
	☐ use the simple past negative to ask and answer questions about the past.	page 47
FUNCTIONAL LANGUAGE	☐ congratulate and sympathize with people.	page 48
	☐ check my understanding.	page 49
SKILLS	☐ write responses to comments about experiences.	page 51
	☐ agree and disagree.	page 51

UNIT 6 BUY NOW, PAY LATER

6.1 BLACK FRIDAY FUN

1 VOCABULARY: Using money

A **Complete the sentences with the correct form of the verbs in the box.**

borrow	cost	lend	save
~~sell~~	shop online	spend	waste

1 That store is _____selling_____ TVs at a very good price. They _____ very little money. My brother asked me to _____ him some money so he can buy one. I want to get one, too!

2 I _____ money from Davon to buy a few video games on Black Friday. But that day, I _____ a lot of money. I need to save money now!

3 Yes, ma'am you can buy two sweaters for the price of one and _____ half on the final price.

4 My wife likes to _____ – she loves the internet! She bought two dresses online, but they were too small. That was a _____ of time!

2 GRAMMAR: *be going to*

A **Put the words in the correct order to make sentences and questions.**

1 new / order / to / I'm / the / going / video game.

I'm going to order the new video game.

2 sell / going / Cara / is / her / to / car.

_____

3 pay / to / you / me / Are / going / back?

_____

4 all that / to / spend / going / Is / she / money?

_____

5 aren't / they / going / to / money / No, / waste / on that.

_____

6 bank / going / me / lend / The / isn't / to / the money.

_____

42

B **Look at the to-do list. Then write sentences.**

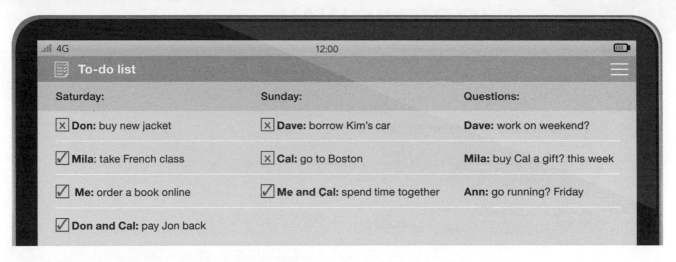

4G	12:00	
To-do list		
Saturday:	**Sunday:**	**Questions:**
☒ **Don:** buy new jacket	☒ **Dave:** borrow Kim's car	**Dave:** work on weekend?
☑ **Mila:** take French class	☒ **Cal:** go to Boston	**Mila:** buy Cal a gift? this week
☑ **Me:** order a book online	☑ **Me and Cal:** spend time together	**Ann:** go running? Friday
☑ **Don and Cal:** pay Jon back		

1 Don isn't going to buy a new jacket on Saturday.
2 Mila _____
3 I _____
4 Don and Cal _____
5 Dave _____
6 Cal _____
7 Cal and I _____
8 _____ Dave _____ ?
9 _____ Mila _____ ?
10 _____ Ann _____ ?

3 GRAMMAR AND VOCABULARY

A **What are you doing this weekend? Use the words in the box and *be going to* to write sentences and questions about your weekend. Give information about who, what, when, and where.**

borrow	buy	go to	~~lend~~	order
pay back	sell	spend money on	spend time with	~~work on~~

1 My brother and I are going to work on my motorcycle on Saturday.
2 _____
3 _____
4 _____
5 _____
6 _____
7 _____
8 Is Tony going to lend me his laptop on Friday?
9 _____ ?
10 _____ ?

6.2 SHOP THIS WAY

1 VOCABULARY: Shopping

A **Write each word in the correct category.**

cart	cash register	~~customer~~	department store	drugstore
grocery store	price	sale	sales clerk	shelf

People	Places	Things
customer		

2 GRAMMAR: Determiners

A **Complete the sentences using the determiners in the box.**

all	~~all of~~	many	most	none	some

1 _____All of_____ the stores in town have great prices today.

2 _____ of the customers prefer shopping online – three out of five people say they prefer it.

3 _____ of us like to waste time waiting in line.

4 _____ of them bought new clothes on Friday. They are all very happy.

5 You can save _____ money when the store has a sale.

6 _____ malls are open tonight until midnight. Only one closed early.

B **Correct the sentences.**

1 All department stores in the city have sales.
   All of the department stores in the city have sales.

2 No customers who shop here like the long lines at the cash registers.
   _____

3 Most them are going to borrow money from the bank.
   _____

4 Some of malls are going to offer better discounts.
   _____

5 None sales clerks are very friendly today.
   _____

6 Many the sales signs in this store have the wrong information.
   _____

3 GRAMMAR AND VOCABULARY

A Imagine you are the manager of a grocery store. You want to know what your customers think about your store. Complete the questions to ask customers about shopping there. Use the determiners, words, and phrases in the boxes.

all	many	most	some

| cash registers | groceries | sales people | sale signs |
| shelves | shopping carts | the store | |

1 Were _____ most of the sales clerks _____ friendly?

2 Did _____ have correct information?

3 Were _____ broken?

4 Did _____ prices on them?

5 Were _____ dirty?

6 Do like shopping here _____ time?

B Complete the following sentences with your own answers.

1 Most of the department stores in my town _____

2 None of the department stores in my town _____

3 All of the grocery stores in my town _____

4 Some of the malls in my town _____

5 Many stores in my town _____

6.3 WHAT DO YOU CALL THEM IN ENGLISH?

1 FUNCTIONAL LANGUAGE: Phrases to use when you don't know the word

A **Complete the conversation with the words in the box.**

> call   ~~know~~   like   thing   use

A Hi. Can I help you?

B Yes, please. I'm looking for … I don't
¹_____know_____ the word in English.
It's a ²_____ to connect electronics.

A Hmm … You mean an "adapter"?

B Not exactly. It's ³_____ an adapter,
but you ⁴_____ it to plug in a lot
of devices at once.

A Oh, got it! We do have them. Power strips.

B What do you ⁵_____ them in English?

A Power strips.

B That's right! Thanks!

2 REAL-WORLD STRATEGY: Asking for words in English

A **Read the conversation. Complete it with the correct expressions.**

A Hi, do you need any help?

B Hi, yes. I'm looking for some things. You use them to eat.
How do ¹_____?

A I'm not sure. You mean like spoons?

B No. They're like spoons, but you use them to
cut food. What's ²_____
for them?

A Knives.

B What ³_____ again?

A Knives.

B That's right, thank you.

3　FUNCTIONAL LANGUAGE AND REAL-WORLD STRATEGY

A　You're going to write a conversation. First, look at the pictures below. Find out what the items are called in English – use your dictionary or go online. Write the words under the pictures. Then follow the instructions in exercise B.

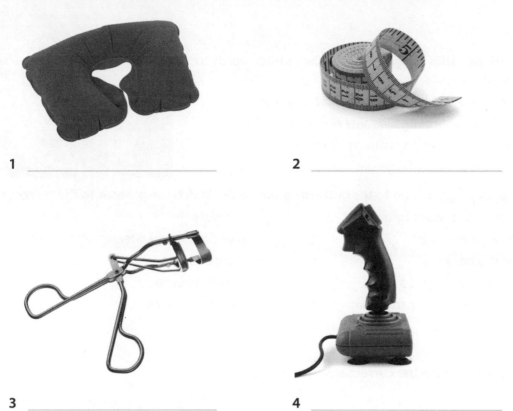

1 _____

2 _____

3 _____

4 _____

B　Before you write the conversation, complete the chart with expressions you plan to use.

Offering to help	
Explaining your language problem	
Explaining the function of the thing you want	
Asking the name in English	
Saying you understand	

C　Write your conversation with the expressions from exercise B.

A　Hi. _____ ?

B　Yes, please. I'm looking for … I _____ .
　　It's _____ .

A　What is it for?

B　You _____ .

A　Ah! I _____ ! _____ .

B　What _____ ?

A　_____ .

B　That's right. Thanks!

MONEY LESSONS

LISTENING

A 🔊 6.01 **Listen to the radio program. Circle the correct words to complete the sentences.**

1 The program is about *street markets / smart shopping*.

2 The speaker thinks shopping lists *are / aren't* a good idea.

3 It *is / is not* a good idea to pay with credit cards.

4 It's a good idea to *never / always* save every time you shop.

B 🔊 6.01 **LISTEN FOR DETAIL** **Listen to the radio program again. Match the phrases to the correct topic.**

1 Know how much you want to spend.
2 Credit cards are dangerous.
3 Put a little in the bank.
4 You lose nothing when you ask.
5 Write down what you need and want.

a _____ Use cash.
b _____ Save first, spend later.
c _____ Make a list.
d __1__ Decide a number.
e _____ Discuss the price.

2 READING

A **Read the blog post. Choose the correct answers below.**

> ● ● ● ◀ ▶   🔍 🏠
>
> My trip to Rio is going to be amazing! I can't wait to go shopping there! Brazilians dress well, so I always check what's in their stores.
>
> Gilson Martins is a large store in Rio. Sometimes international movie stars shop there! Now, be careful because, as Brazilians say: *A única coisa fácil sobre o dinheiro e perdê-lo*. It means that the only easy thing about money is losing it. Prices in this store are high, and you can spend lots of money in just one visit.
>
> Perhaps my favorite shopping trip was on my last visit there. I went to the street markets in Ipanema. I found nice leather bags and beautiful pictures. I was careful with what I bought because Brazilians also say: *O barato sai caro*: Cheap things can be very expensive.
>
> I am going to have so much fun shopping! But I also plan not to spend a lot because: *Dinheiro não dá em árvores*. Money doesn't grow on trees!

1 What kind of blog is this?

  a a travel blog   **b** a work blog   **c** a business blog

2 What does the writer enjoy in Rio?

  a movie stars   **b** fashion   **c** shopping

3 Why does the writer say that cheap things from street markets can be expensive?

  a Because they aren't always very good.   **b** Because you can buy them only in Brazil.

  c Because you can't return them.

4 Why does the writer say that money doesn't grow on trees?

  a Money is hard to get, so don't waste it.   **b** Money is hard to find in Brazil.

  c Shopping is difficult work.

3 WRITING

A **Rewrite the sentences using *one / ones* and *it*.**

1 Movie stars are the <u>famous people</u> that shop there.
_____

2 Ipanema's street market is great. I can't wait to visit <u>my favorite market</u> again.
_____

3 There are many stores in Rio. Gilson Martins is a famous <u>store</u>.
_____

4 Of all the countries, Brazil is the <u>country</u> I'm in love with.
_____

5 Brazilians are the <u>people</u> that dress well.
_____

B **Here is something else Brazilians say:** *Quanto mais se tem, mais se quer.* **It means: The more you have, the more you want. Write a vlog script explaining the meaning of this saying in English. When would you use this saying? Use *ones* and *it*.**

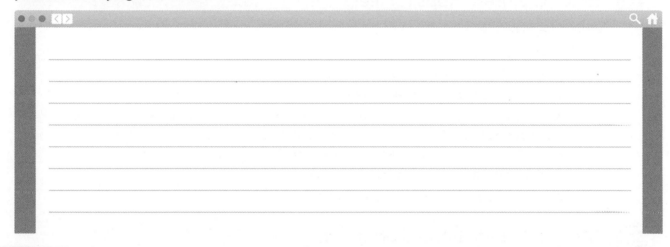

CHECK AND REVIEW

Read the statements. Can you do these things?

UNIT 6	Mark the boxes. ☑ I can do it. ? I am not sure.		If you are not sure, go back to these pages in the Student's Book.
	I can …		
VOCABULARY	☐ use money words.		page 54
	☐ use shopping words.		page 56
GRAMMAR	☐ use *be going to* to talk about future plans.		page 55
	☐ use determiners to talk about quantity.		page 57
FUNCTIONAL LANGUAGE	☐ use phrases to say what I want when I don't know the word.		page 58
	☐ ask how to say something in English.		page 59
SKILLS	☐ write a vlog script.		page 61
	☐ use *it* and *ones*.		page 61

EXTRA ACTIVITIES

1 TIME TO SPEAK Things you have in common

A **Find out about things you have in common with your friends and family.**

- Write some questions. See examples below:

  When is your birthday?

  How many brothers and sisters do you have?

  What city are your parents from?

  Where are your grandparents from?

- Add more questions to the list above.

- Post the questions to your social media account, or email them to friends and family.

- Create a private group and invite your friends and family members.

B **Ask your friends and family to answer the questions. Make a list of things that you have in common with them.**

2 TIME TO SPEAK Apps for life

A **Write an app review.**

- Look at the apps on your phone.

- Make a list of the three apps that you use the most.

- Select your favorite out of the three.

- Write: 1) what is good and not so good about that app, 2) how the app helps you with your daily life, 3) what changes you want to see in future versions. Use the expressions from the unit to express your opinions and give examples.

- Go to an app store and find the app's page.

- Write a review of the app using your ideas.

3 TIME TO SPEAK Fitness programs

A **Choose a couple of gyms or sports clubs that you know of or like. Go online. Find out about their fitness programs. Compare the fitness programs in both places and decide which one is better for you. Recommend the place you selected to your classmates at the next class. Explain your reasons.**

4 TIME TO SPEAK The gift of giving

A **Imagine you want to give a small gift to a friend living in another country.**

- Write about what she or he likes to wear and do.

- Call her or him or contact her/him online and ask about his/her interests and hobbies.

- Make a list of possible gifts that are typical of your country or region.

- Decide what gift is the best. Think of something unusual and attractive.

B **Make a decision about the gift for your friend and explain it in the next class.**

5 TIME TO SPEAK Iceberg!

A **Read the fact file below. Research more facts online about the life of this *Titanic* survivor.**

Name	Lawrence Beesley
Birthdate	December 31, 1877
Nationality	British
Age	35 years old
Occupation	Science teacher
Author of	*The Loss of the SS Titanic*
Death	February 14, 1967
Quote	"… it was easy to lose one's way on the *Titanic*."

B **Write the story of Lawrence Beesley. Use the facts you know about him to write a short description of his life.**

C **Present your story at the next class.**

6 TIME TO SPEAK Eureka!

A **Go online and find an invention that you like. Find out about:**
- what problem it solves.
- when it was invented.
- how much the product costs.

B **Write a report about the invention and bring it to the next class. Explain it and discuss it with the rest of the class.**

NOTES

The authors and publishers acknowledge the following sources of copyright material and are grateful for the permissions granted. While every effort has been made, it has not always been possible to identify the sources of all the material used, or to trace all copyright holders. If any omissions are brought to our notice, we will be happy to include the appropriate acknowledgements on reprinting and in the next update to the digital edition, as applicable.

Photography credits
Key: B = Below, BG = Background, BL = Below Left, BR = Below Right, C = Centre, CL = Centre Left, CR = Centre Right, T = Top, TC = Top Centre, TL = Top Left, TR = Top Right.

All images are sourced from Getty Images.

p. 2 (BG): aldomurillo/E+; p. 2 (couple): Antonio_Diaz/iStock/Getty Images Plus; p. 4 (keychain): Michael Zwahlen/EyeEm; p. 4 (brush): Ghrzuzudu/iStock/Getty Images Plus; p. 4 (umbrella): macrovector/ iStock/Getty Images Plus; p. 6 (BG): Caiaimage/Sam Edwards; p. 7: Westend61; p. 8: Elke Meitzel/Cultura; p. 10: T3 Magazine/Future; p. 12 (photo 1): Topic Images Inc.; p. 12 (photo 2): Shannon Fagan/ DigitalVision; p. 12 (photo 3): Image Source; p. 12 (photo 4): pixhook/ E+; p. 12 (photo 5): Zocha_K/E+; p. 12 (photo 6): bagi1998/E+; p. 14 (CL): Tom Grill/Photographer's Choice RF; p. 14 (CR): markgoddard/ iStock/Getty Images Plus; p. 15: Caner CANDEMIR/iStock/Getty Images Plus; p. 16: Kelvin Murray/Stone; p. 18 (LED): fredrocko/E+; p. 18 (tennis player): PeopleImages/DigitalVision; p. 18 (soccer): vgajic/E+; p. 18 (field): adventtr/iStock/Getty Images Plus; p. 18 (goal): Cocoon/ DigitalVision; p. 18 (court): David Madison/DigitalVision; p. 18 (race): Hero Images; p. 18 (pool): baona/iStock/Getty Images Plus; p. 18 (athlete): Milk & Honey Creative/Stone; p. 18: (fans): LeoPatrizi/E+; p. 18 (gym): XiXinXing; p. 20 (TL): alvarez/E+; p. 20 (TC): Robert Llewellyn/ Photolibrary; p. 20 (TR): Ariel Skelley/DigitalVision; p. 21: gilaxia/ iStock/Getty Images Plus; p. 22 (TL): Handout/Getty Images Sport; p. 22 (TR): Jeff Greenberg/Universal Images Group; p. 24: ©fitopardo. com/Moment; p. 25: Jeff Greenberg/Universal Images Group; p. 27: PeopleImages/E+; p. 28: Maximilian Stock Ltd/Photographer's Choice; p. 29 (CL): stevezmina1/DigitalVision Vectors; p. 29 (C): kimberrywood/ DigitalVision Vectors; p. 29 (CR): KristinaVelickovic/DigitalVision Vectors; p. 29 (B): Dougal Waters/DigitalVision; p. 30: Peter Cade/The Image Bank; p. 31 (TL): TonySoh/DigitalVision Vectors; p. 31 (TC): nico_blue/DigitalVision Vectors; p. 31 (TR): Leontura/DigitalVision Vectors; p. 32: Jim Rankin/Toronto Star; p. 33: MIKE NELSON/AFP; p. 35: Mike Powell/DigitalVision; p. 36: Peter Dazeley/Photographer's Choice; p. 37 (TR): Pictorial Parade/Archive Photos; p. 37 (BR): Stuart Franklin – FIFA; p. 38 (T): Commercial Eye/The Image Bank; p. 38 (BR): pshonka/iStock/Getty Images Plus; p. 39 (TR): ZU_09/DigitalVision Vectors; p. 40 (BR): Marcelo Endelli/LatinContent WO; p. 40 (TR): Yadid Levy/robertharding; p. 42 (TV): Cobalt88/iStock/Getty Images Plus; p. 42 (console): Jane_Kelly/iStock/Getty Images Plus; p. 42 (sweater): Mark Murphy/DigitalVision Vectors; p. 42 (cart): johavel/iStock/Getty Images Plus; p. 46 (TR): andresr/E+; p. 46 (powerbar): LongHa2006/E+; p. 46 (BR): Yagi Studio/Taxi; p. 47 (joystick): Emanuele Ravecca/EyeEm; p. 47 (eyelash): Steve Wisbauer/Stockbyte; p. 47 (tape): sergeyskleznev/iStock/ Getty Images Plus; p. 47 (pillow): ChamilleWhite/iStock/Getty Images Plus; p. 48: Roy JAMES Shakespeare/The Image Bank;

Front cover photography by Alija/E+/Getty Images.

Illustration
Dusan Lakicevic (Beehive illustration) p. 13; Liav Zabari (Lemonade illustration) pp. 19, 39.

Audio
Audio production by CityVox, New York.

Corpus
Development of this publication has made use of the Cambridge English Corpus (CEC). The CEC is a multi-billion word collection of contemporary spoken and written English. It includes British English, American English, and other varieties. It also includes the Cambridge Learner Corpus, the world's biggest collection of learner writing, developed in collaboration with Cambridge Assessment. Cambridge University Press uses the CEC to provide evidence about language use that helps to produce better language teaching materials.

Our *Evolve* authors study the Corpus to see how English is really used, and to identify typical learner mistakes. This information informs the authors' selection of vocabulary, grammar items and Student's Book Corpus features such as the Accuracy Check, Register Check, and Insider English